For my family--

on both sides of the river

Bloom Tunes:

Poems for Spring

Julie Krantz

Wake-Up Call

Spring is when the world unfolds,

wriggles free of frost and cold,

strips away its hoary sheets,

stretches legs, arches feet,

scatters seeds in winter's bed,

lightly shakes its tousled head,

reaches arms toward summer skies,

catches rainclouds flying by.

rubs its eyes with mossy fists,

kisses earth with dew and mist.

Buttercup

A buttercup

in Lily's lap

is like

a scoop

of sun.

A lily in

a briar patch

is butter

on a bun.

A Snail's Tail

he

wears

a

shell

upon

his

back.

antlers black.

His feet are slimy,

he leaves a trail

wherever he goes . . .

Nighty-night!

'course where that is

no one knows!

But though he slides

on feet of lead,

he's always first to climb in bed!

Traveling South

Yellow daisies
line the tracks,
sunny pinpoints
smiling back.

whistle blowing,
engine fast,
stalwart lilies
sailing past.

maples rim
the river's mouth,
slender fingers
pointing south.

frilly caps of
Queen Anne's lace
crown the hills
with bridal grace.

you and I
sit side by side
as this showy
world drifts by.

holding hands
and bowing heads,
we pray springtime
never ends.

Moneybags

I have a million dollars

tucked beneath my bed.

my brother calls me

'moneybags,'

and says it's in my head.

but I've never

spent a quarter--

or even fifteen cents--

and I swear

I saw it yesterday--

just don't know

where it went!

Loosey Toothy

My tooth is loose,

    my gum is sore,

I just can't take it anymore.

    a wiggle left,

      a jiggle right,

I'll get it out

    in one more bite.

But suddenly

    I'm full of dread.

My wiggle-finger's

    turning red.

I think it's blood--

    but I'm not sure--

until I see it
    on the floor.
my gore has turned
    the carpet brown!

I grab a towel
    and swab it 'round.
but what a mess
    is on that rug--

morsels, crumbs,
    a million bugs.
that's when I find--
    to my surprise--
my baby tooth
    among the fries.

Favorites

Running, jumping,

skipping, too,

they're my favorite

things to do.

but when

my dad and I

play catch,

that's the 'doing'

I like best!

CRITTER FRITTERS

Snort

Brown eyes,
big ears,
soft black coat.

see you
on the hillside,
grazing with
the goats.

do you like
your grasses tall,
or do you like
them short?

and do you simply
moo all day--
or do you
like to snort?

>>>

Cow

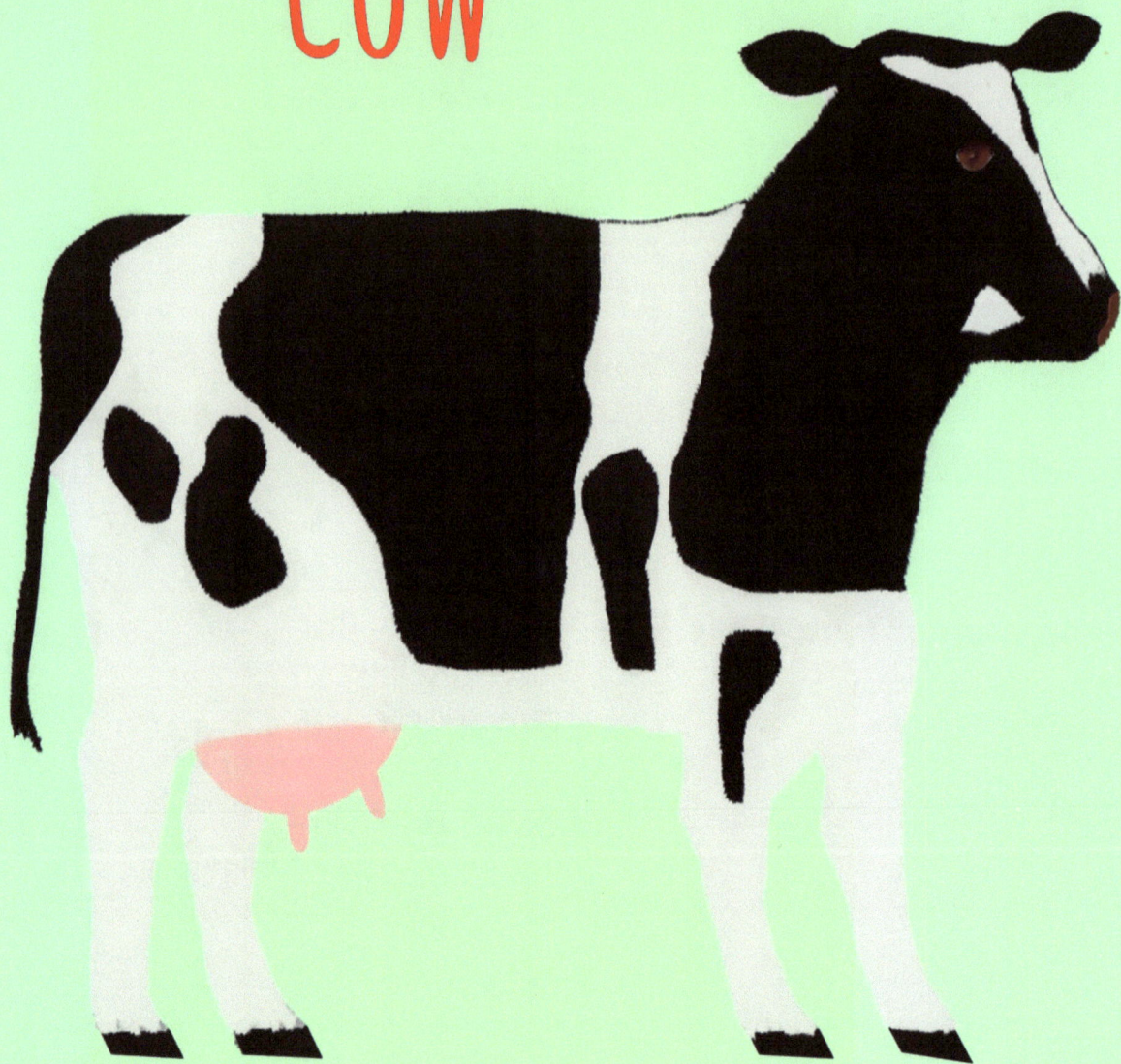

Rockstar

Slippy,

slimy,

little guy,

sitting on a rock.

what is it

you're thinking

when you

croak,

croak,

croak

non-stop?

>>>

FROG

Flit

He flits

he flaps

he flies all night,

he never

seems to mellow--

unless,

of course,

he spies

a light

that's white

or cream

or yellow.

>>>

Moth

Little Bit

Little climber
on a limb
you're tiny
as a rat.
when you flick
your pointy ears,
I think you are
part bat!

you sleep all day
and play all night,
inside your woody pen.
I hope you can
go home someday--
though when you do,
I'll miss you, friend.

>>>

LEMUR

Growler

Onions, olives, pickles, pears--
my stomach is a fiend, I swear!
I feed it morning,
noon, and night,
but all it wants
is "one more bite."
no matter what is on my plate,
my tummy craves another taste!
so if my eating never ends,
it's not for me--
it's for my 'friend.'

Opposites

On soft warm earth

the blackbird swoops

to nip a

tasty worm.

on cold wet snow

the reindeer stoops

to taste a

nippy fern.

A Panoply of Canopy

Trees like umbrellas

splatter the sky,

giant green goggles

for god's sunny eye.

verdant in summer,

red-tipped in spring,

waving their branches

like birds on the wing.

Home Sweet Home

Heads 'n Toes

My tummy aches,

    I'm not surprised--

why did I eat

    a thousand fries?

but ten little sodas

    all in a row

    made me hungry

    head to toe

so I ate a stack of burgers

and a hill of baked beans.

then I washed it all down

with a tub of ice cream.

Measurements

How Many?

How many rainstorms
does it take
to widen puddles
into lakes?

How much?

and just how hot
must deserts get
before their cacti
start to sweat?

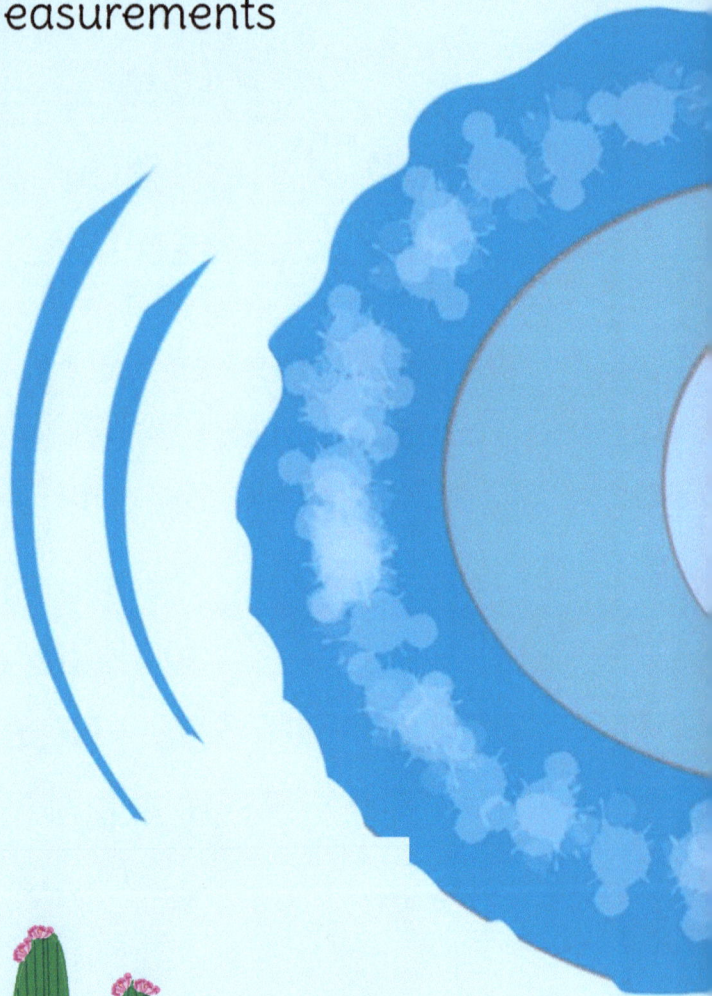

How Long?

How long does
a flower last
before it starts
to wither?

and how long
must a snakelet grow
until it starts
to slither?

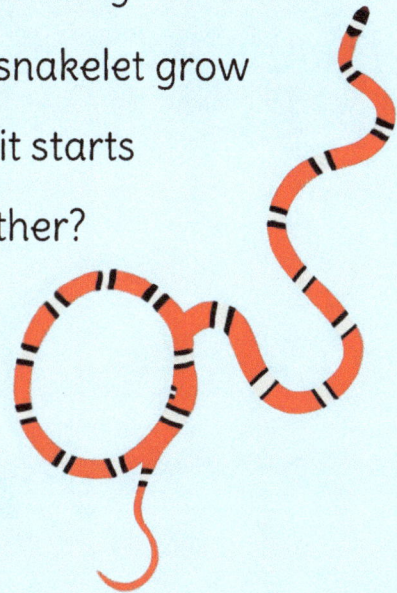

Wanted . . .

One rabbit hole--
not too muddy,
not too deep--
suitable for a young girl's
slipping, sliding, falling

d
  o
    w
     n

to another world
where all is
whimsical, wild,
and wonderful--
and she herself
is

magic.

Bloom Tune

When trees

turn green

and bluebirds call,

we nestle winter

in with fall.

The bulbs we set

in loamy beds

poke through earth

and nod their heads.

Author's Note . . .

If by chance

this little book

should find it's way

to you,

please pick it up

and dust it off,

enjoy it

and review.

Thank you--jgk

Also by this author . . .

Isabel Plum: Ichthyologist

Tip & Oliver: BFFs

Blueberry Moon

YOGABETS:
An Acrobatic Alphabet

Sweet Feet:
Love Poems for Little Peeps

Un Chat Charmant:
One Charming Cat

Sledding Down the Hill:
Poems for Winter

Stella Bellarosa:
Tales of an Aspiring Teenage Superhero

2016

www.amazon.com/Julie-Krantz/e/B00996YNZ4

www.ingramcontent.com/pod-product-compliance
Lightning Source LLC
Chambersburg PA
CBHW041220040426

42443CB00002B/28